THE
SHEPHERD
KING

The Rise, Reign, and Redemption of David

Lifeway Press®
Brentwood, Tennessee

ISBN 978-1-0877-6740-6
Item 005838145
Dewey Decimal Classification Number: 242
Subject Heading: DEVOTIONAL LITERATURE / BIBLE STUDY AND TEACHING / GOD

Printed in the United States of America

Student Ministry Publishing
Lifeway Resources
200 Powell Place, Suite 100
Brentwood, TN, 37027-7707

We believe that the Bible has God for its author; salvation for its end; and truth, without any mixture of error, for its matter and that all Scripture is totally true and trustworthy. To review Lifeway's doctrinal guideline, please visit www.lifeway.com/doctrinalguideline.

Unless otherwise noted, all Scripture quotations are taken from the Christian Standard Bible®, Copyright © 2017 by Holman Bible Publishers. Used by permission. Christian Standard Bible® and CSB® are federally registered trademarks of Holman Bible Publishers.

PUBLISHING TEAM

Director, Student Ministry
Ben Trueblood

Manager, Student Ministry Publishing
John Paul Basham

Editorial Team Leader
Karen Daniel

Writer
Leslie Hudson

Content Editor
Kyle Wiltshire

Production Editor
April-Lyn Caouette

Graphic Designer
Shiloh Stufflebeam

TABLE OF CONTENTS

INTRO

You may have picked up this book and thought, "I already know about David"—and maybe you're right. You probably know about David and Goliath, David's friendship with Jonathan, and David becoming king of Israel. But few students look deeply into David's story because it takes two whole books of the Old Testament to tell it! In the Bible, we first meet David when he's a teenager, and we can follow the story all the way through to his death. Few people get that kind of thorough detail in God's Word.

In carefully observing David's life, we get to peer into the many layers of this famous man: the good and the bad, the successes and the failures, the moments of greatness as well as his shame. Quite honestly, most of us wouldn't want our life story to be published in this much detail! Most of us don't want everyone knowing all of our secrets and the mistakes we've made.

In studying David, we actually are able to look into ourselves and our relationship with God: what it means to be chosen, how we should live as we obediently wait, and how a godly leader walks through decades of life. Because we start in David's teenage years, you've picked up this book at just the right time. For the next thirty days, pretend that David is your favorite uncle, who just sat down next to you and asked, "Did I ever tell you about the time . . ." Listen as he pours his heart out without exaggerating or being fake. That same uncle would want you to hear his life story, learn from his mistakes, and believe him when he teaches you truths you can count on.

"Uncle David" would tell you that God's favor and love were poured out lavishly on his life through every situation and in every season. Ultimately, this isn't a story about David, but a story about God. And it's the story of how God took a teenager—just like you—and stuck with him forever.

Getting Started

*This devotional contains thirty days of content, broken down into sections. Each day is divided into three elements—**discover**, **delight**, and **display**—to help you grow in your faith.*

discover

This section helps you examine the passage in light of who God is and determine what it says about your identity in relationship to Him. Included here is the daily Scripture reading and key verses, along with illustrations and commentary to guide you as you learn more about God's Word.

delight

In this section, you'll be challenged by questions and activities that help you see how God is alive and active in every detail of His Word and your life.

display

Here's where you take action. This section calls you to apply what you've learned through each day.

Each day also includes a prayer activity at the conclusion of the devotion.

Throughout the devotional, you'll also find extra items to help you connect with the topic personally, such as Scripture memory verses, additional resources, and interactive articles.

DAVID'S

SECTION 1

RISE

When David first entered the story of Scripture, he was just a teenage boy. God had rejected Saul and chose David to replace him as King of Israel. Sounds like a straightforward plot, right? Well, not so fast! Saul didn't leave the throne easily, and God's plan took years to unfold. If you've ever had a person who didn't like you no matter how loyal you were to them, these Scriptures will speak to you.

HE'S THE ONE

discover

READ 1 SAMUEL 16.

> But the LORD said to Samuel, "Do not look at his
> appearance or his stature because I have rejected him.
> Humans do not see what the LORD sees, for humans
> see what is visible, but the LORD sees the heart."
> — 1 Samuel 16:7

You know that emoji of a face with two eyes, bulging out, shocked at the words on the phone? That's the image you may have in mind for the awkward situations in today's verses. First, the prophet Samuel was (justifiably) afraid to go anoint a new king because he knew that the current king, Saul, might kill him. God told him to go anyway. (Picture that emoji.) Samuel obediently followed God's instruction, and went to offer a sacrifice as he waited to hear God's choice for a new king. Jesse's oldest son walked in, looking like a million bucks; Samuel was certain that this was the one. But God disagreed, assuring the old prophet that He was less concerned with strong arms and a broad chin and was more in favor of a soft heart. (Picture the emoji again.)

All of Jesse's sons passed by, but God was silent in the prophet Samuel's mind. Samuel then asked an awkward question: "Is it possible you might have forgotten someone, Jesse?" He had. The youngest son had been left at home because someone had to keep the sheep safe. Surely God wouldn't want the youngest! Turns out, He did.

Whether David knew it or not, taking care of sheep would prepare him for God's ultimate plan for him: to be the shepherd of God's people. But it wasn't the sheep that made him the right man for the job—it was his heart. God saw a heart that was ready to be yielded to His plan.

delight

God's choosing David was unexpected to his father and to the prophet Samuel. When was a time when you've been surprised by God's choice in your life?

How is David described in these verses? What about him is *not* described? What else did God know about him that others couldn't see (see v. 7)?

display

David wasn't ready to be king in his teenage years, but God could still see that his heart was on the right path. You may have no idea what your future looks like, but God's plan for you involves a heart that is tender toward Him. Without intentional heart preparation, you'll miss the blessing of walking the path God has for you. Take time today to check your heart. Are you allowing God to shape it through His Word? Use the prayer prompt below to write out your heart's desire, and take some intentional steps to ready your heart for whatever He has in store for you.

As you pray today, invite the Holy Spirit to give you an honest assessment of your own heart. Is it soft and open, ready to receive God's love and instruction? Is it hard and shut closed, refusing to believe God's Word? Pray David's words from Psalm 51:10 aloud to close your prayer.

THE CHAMP AND THE ROOKIE

discover

READ 1 SAMUEL 17.

David said to the Philistine, "You come against me with a sword, spear, and javelin, but I come against you in the name of the LORD of Armies, the God of the ranks of Israel—you have defied him."
— 1 Samuel 17:45

If you're a fan of action movies, today's reading probably plays like a great battle scene in your mind. We see two armies, separated by a ravine, facing one another. The Philistine army has a great champion, Goliath, who had been "a warrior since he was young" (v. 33). You can hear Goliath's booming voice calling for a challenger, and from the opposing force—the Israelites—you hear . . . crickets.

This was a pretty typical way to fight back then: one army's best fighter versus the other's best in order to determine the winning side. But there was a problem: the biggest, strongest fighter for the Israelites was the king, Saul. And he wasn't volunteering. Though Saul had been a mighty warrior, he wanted nothing to do with Goliath. Feeding off of his fear, none of the other men seemed to want to tangle with the big man, either.

David wasn't even there to fight; he'd come to bring food to his brothers in the army. But when he heard the challenge of the giant Goliath, he was insulted—not for himself or his people, but for his God. David didn't have the skills, or the gear, or the size, but he had the heart and the confidence that God would bring victory.

delight

What were some things David was risking by taking a stand against the giant Goliath?

What does David's willingness to stand up for God reveal about his faith?

How did David's words encourage those who were watching and listening?

display

David stood up against Goliath when no one else in Israel—not even their king—was willing to. We need to stand firm in our faith and convictions, even if we stand alone. We are called to believe God, but we are also called to act on that belief: speaking up for the voiceless, defending the weak, befriending the lonely, and boldly confronting evil. In James 2:14-26, we read that faith without works isn't really faith at all. God is calling us to be bold as we take a step of faith—not because we're courageous, but because He is faithful. In the space below, write one way you can boldly put your faith into action this week.

Lord, I don't face Goliath, but I definitely have big challenges and big fears. Sometimes it seems like there is no way I can battle all the things that stand against You. But I also know that the battle is Yours; I can be brave because You give me victory.

DAY 3

THE GOLDEN TOUCH

discover

READ 1 SAMUEL 18.

**Every time the Philistine commanders came out to
fight, David was more successful than all of Saul's
officers. So his name became well known.**
— 1 Samuel 18:30

There's an old story about a man named Midas who had a "golden touch": everything he touched turned to gold.[1] In today's chapter, David didn't turn everything into gold, but he did have an amazing run of success. He developed a deep friendship with Saul's son Jonathan. (You can read more about him in 1 Samuel 14.) Jonathan went out of his way to befriend David, pledging his allegiance and loyalty to the man God had chosen to be king, even though his father was currently serving in that role (which meant Jonathan would normally have been next in line for the throne).

On top of that, the people loved David and gave him accolades, even when it angered Saul. David was successful in battle and in the eyes of people. Through all this success, Saul's plans to kill David were thwarted each time.

But we'd be wrong to believe that David's leadership skills or fighting abilities were the reason for his success. His victories came because God granted them—God was the source of David's life path. In trusting God's plan, David could walk in confidence that God would be the source of his power and victory as he journeyed.

[1] "King Midas and his touch," Greeka, accessed November 17, 2022, https://www.greeka.com/greece-myths/king-midas/.

delight

From what you've read of David's life so far, what were some difficulties God allowed into his life?

What were some life lessons David learned by going through these trying years?

display

Just as God was shaping David's life path, providing struggles as well as victory, He shapes ours as well. In struggle as well as in victory, we can trust the plan of our all-knowing, always-loving, almighty Father. God's Word can give you guidance and encouragement in your struggles, and it will keep you focused on God's glory in your triumph. Start a list of Scriptures that will keep you God-honoring and God-glorifying in the good, the bad, the hard, and the victorious. Jot them in a notebook and keep it with your Bible, ready to be used as a mighty weapon (see Eph. 6:17).

As you pray today, confess to God any fears you have about the future. He can handle your honesty! Allow His message of peace to fill your heart and mind as you choose to believe truth about Him. He is with you; He has a plan for your life. He is in control, and He will guide you through today, tomorrow, and every day for the rest of your life.

UNEXPECTED RESCUES

discover

READ 1 SAMUEL 19.

When it was reported to Saul that David was at Naioth in Ramah, he sent agents to seize David. However, when they saw the group of prophets prophesying with Samuel leading them, the Spirit of God came on Saul's agents, and they also started prophesying.
— 1 Samuel 19:19-20

Today's verses give us deep insight into King Saul: his torment led him to irrational, unbalanced thoughts and actions. David was the commander of Saul's army, his son's best friend, his daughter's husband, and his private musician; yet over and over, Saul attempted to kill him! Saul couldn't see the blessings that David had brought into his life. He saw only the threat that David would unseat him from the throne.

It would have been easy for David to lose hope; after all, what could he do against a man who was such an unpredictable king? But God provided rescue for David, over and over, in a variety of ways. First, Jonathan's wise words to his father inspired Saul to undo his edict to have David killed. (Unfortunately, that vow didn't last.) Next, God gave David the nimble body to avoid Saul's spear. When Saul sent agents to murder David, God simply sent His Spirit into them and gave them the temporary job of prophet!

God didn't work in the same way every time that David needed to be rescued from Saul, but God faithfully kept him safe each time his life was in danger.

delight

David was blessed with loyal friends. Who are your loyal friends? How do they push you to be more like Jesus?

What does the Holy Spirit causing Saul and his men to start prophesying reveal about the power of the Spirit?

display

Just as David experienced the blessing of friends in the midst of trouble, we can too. Perhaps you have a friend or family member who listens when you vent, sits next to you every day in science class, or cheers you on in your struggles. Don't minimize those relationships—they are a blessing from God and proof of His hand in your life. We should regularly thank God for our friends, but today why don't you also acknowledge them personally? Thank a few of your friends today for their friendship, and recognize their words and actions that help and encourage you.

In your prayer time today, thank God for the people who help you and love you. Then take a moment to offer your own friendship: ask God to show you a few people who could use an encouraging word, a kind smile, or a hand of help.

DAY 5

A TOUGH CHOICE

discover

READ 1 SAMUEL 20.

**Jonathan then said to David, "Go in the assurance the
two of us pledged in the name of the Lord when we
said, 'The Lord will be a witness between you and me
and between my offspring and your offspring forever.'"
Then David left, and Jonathan went into the city.
— 1 Samuel 20:42**

Jonathan and David were the best of friends, to be sure. But it was more
than that: Jonathan had "bound [himself] to David in close friendship,
and loved him as much as he loved himself" (1 Sam. 18:1). Jonathan had
also pledged his future military allegiance to David (see 1 Sam. 18:3-4)
and had stood up for David to his father. Think about that implication:
Jonathan was the king's son, officially the next in line to be ruler. If he
had joined forces with Saul, he could have secured his spot as the
next king.

But that's not how God-honoring, genuine friendship works. Jonathan
wasn't concerned with his own future; he had entrusted it to the Lord.
Jonathan was also willing to sacrifice his sure-fire chance at being king so
that he could honor his word to David.

When David asked Jonathan for the big favor in today's reading,
Jonathan had to choose between his father and his friend. But we see
from Jonathan's words that he didn't struggle with the decision: he
held strong to his pledge to David and to the Lord. His loyalty clearly
revealed his heart and his love.

delight

Jonathan revealed his friendship to David very clearly. How did David show friendship to Jonathan in return?

What are ways you can show healthy loyalty and support to your friends like Jonathan did for David?

display

One of the greatest desires we all share as humans is for genuine, honorable, devoted friends. Although we probably won't find this kind of friend in every season of life, we can always practice being a good friend to others. What are the characteristics of friendship you see exemplified in David and Jonathan? Write those in the space below or in a journal, and then give yourself an honest grade for each characteristic. Jot some ideas for how you can be a better friend, either today or in the future.

Before you pray today, read what Jesus wrote about friendship in John 15:12-15. Take time to thank God for allowing you to have a holy, amazing friendship with Jesus. Consider how He has given this definition for being a friend, and confess the times you weren't a friend to Jesus.

DAY 6

WHEN YOU'VE GOTTA GO

discover

READ 1 SAMUEL 24.

"May the LORD judge between me and you, and may the LORD take vengeance on you for me, but my hand will never be against you."
— 1 Samuel 24:12

In yesterday's Scripture reading, Jonathan sent David away to save him from the wrath of Saul. The next few chapters describe how David was forced to flee to different cities and narrowly escaped death at the hands of Saul, who was becoming more and more paranoid every day.

As today's reading opens, Saul heard that David was hiding near En-gedi, so he assembled 3000 men to kill David. As you might expect from any long trip, eventually Saul needed to make a pit stop, so he went into a cave to relive himself. He didn't realize David and his fugitive friends were in there.

The friends encouraged David to kill Saul—this was his chance! Hadn't God sent Samuel to anoint David? Didn't Saul deserve it for trying to kill David? David didn't follow his friends' advice to kill Saul, but he did cut off the corner of Saul's robe. Even that little act caused David to feel guilt; after all, Saul, like David, had been chosen by God to be king. God had instructed David to wait for the throne, not to take it by force. So, David revealed his actions, confessed his sin, and swore he wouldn't harm Saul.

delight

What is something God convicted you for doing, something others might think is a little thing but that you knew was wrong to do?

Saul was all over the place emotionally. How can you imitate David's behavior toward unpredictable people in your own life?

display

There is never a time when God permits his people to disobey: not if the other person started it, not if they deserve it, not even if you're hangry. Nope—we are called to obey God and wait for His perfect timing, regardless of the situation or the people involved. In the waiting obedience, we learn to trust God, depend on Him, submit to Him, and yield to Him. In the space below or in a journal, write the words: "In every situation, God calls me to . . ." and complete that statement with a list of actions. Here are few to get started: *love, forgive, be patient, practice discernment,* and *share.*

As you pray, consider the different ways you have seen David show integrity in his relationship with Jonathan as well as in his relationship with Saul. In good and bad situations, we are all called to glorify God. Invite God to show you how you can point others to him through the way you treat your friends and even your enemies.

MEMORY VERSE
1 Samuel 16:7

But the Lord said to Samuel, "Do not look at his appearance or his stature because I have rejected him. Humans do not see what the Lord sees, for humans see what is visible, but the Lord sees the heart."

ANGER VERSUS WISDOM

discover

READ 1 SAMUEL 25.

**When Abigail saw David, she quickly got off the donkey and knelt
down with her face to the ground and paid homage to David.
— 1 Samuel 25:23**

We've seen David fighting Goliath and showing restraint by not killing
Saul in the cave. But David wasn't perfect, and today's passage reveals
that clearly.

A foolish man, Nabal, had insulted David. We can only imagine that
David was stressed out: he'd been on the run from Saul for years, he had
to balance God's promise that he would be king with waiting for it to
happen, and he had men around him who were ready and eager to fight.
When Nabal insulted David, his anger flared. David and his men picked
up their swords, ready for battle.

Thankfully, the voice of wisdom interceded: Abigail, Nabal's wife,
intercepted David and his men, offering them food and humility. She
spoke wisdom to David, pleading with him not to make a foolish
decision by taking matters into his own hands. Abigail was courageous
to stand between two hot-headed men, and she saved the lives of
countless people that day.

David had allowed his fury to take over his brain; instead of praying
or seeking the Lord, he had responded in haste. Abigail's plea hit him
squarely in the heart, and he realized the wisdom of her words. David
swallowed his pride and turned his army around. When our heart is
tuned to God, we can hear the voice of wisdom even in fierce anger.

delight

When has been a time when you've made an unwise emotional decision? What was the outcome?

When have you been forced to do something brave to help someone else out? What was the result?

display

It's really hard to stop and listen to wisdom when you're angry. Whether you've been insulted, embarrassed, hurt, or confronted, sometimes all we can see is red, and we don't pause to consider the implications of a rash act. In the space below, write about a time when you were overwhelmed with anger. Then, consider the steps you should take when faced with overwhelming anger in the future: First, spend five minutes alone, praying—seek God's Word for wisdom in that situation. Then, talk it over with a wise, godly mentor. As you allow time, the Bible, and words of peace to move through you, you'll see how God would instruct you to act.

As you pray today, make time for considering the situation that makes you most angry. Is it a person, a class, or a topic? Pour out your heart to the Lord, confessing the times when you haven't handled your anger well. Invite Him to lead you in the way of wisdom and peace.

LIVING IN THE GRAY

discover

READ 1 SAMUEL 27.

Now David said to Achish, "If I have found favor with you, let me be given a place in one of the outlying towns, so I can live there. Why should your servant live in the royal city with you?"
— 1 Samuel 27:5

This chapter opens with what might seem like a good idea. David thought to himself, "One of these days I'll be swept away by Saul" (v. 1), so he decided to go live in the land of the Philistines, their enemies. On the surface, it makes sense—Saul wouldn't go into enemy territory to find him. But God had already promised David that he would be king. What seemed like a good idea was actually the result of fear mixed with anxiety and a lack of faith. David might have thought he was clever, but he was living in the gray zone of sin.

So David openly lived in Philistine territory, where he and his men could settle down without fearing for their lives. However, there aren't many jobs for 600 out-of-work fighting men, so they went to nearby villages to steal and murder. David's compromising plan and lack of trust in God had spiraled into out-of-control sin.

On top of that, David had to lie to the Philistine king because his raiding parties weren't just killing people—they were actually killing Philistine people. What had started out as hiding from Saul had turned to lying, stealing, and murder. It's a steep, slippery slope from fearfulness to outright rebellion against God and other people.

delight

Where is David's focus in these opening verses: on God or on himself? How can you tell?

David justified his actions to himself, something we've all been guilty of. How do we avoid making excuses for ourselves to justify our actions and instead live in obedience to God?

display

Sometimes we act like David, and we find ourselves living in fear as we contemplate the future. We think, "One of these days . . ." and we start making plans that are full of fear and anxiety, completely lacking faith in God's plan for our lives. The best way to avoid this path of thinking is to look backwards and see God's faithfulness throughout our lives up to this point. Take a moment and write out a few of the major events of your life. How was God active in that situation? How did He reveal His faithfulness to you then?

A helpful step in looking backwards and seeing God's provision is to spend time every day reading the promises of God in His Word. As you read your Bible each day, be on the lookout for a promise that God will be with you, empower you, lead you, or help you. Write that promise on an index card or in a prayer notebook, and read through it regularly to remind yourself of His faithfulness.

As you pray today, prepare to spend a few minutes in silence. Open your prayer time by asking, "Lord, where am I living in a gray area? Where am I living sinfully?" Then sit in silence, listening for God's voice speaking to you, and be ready to obey what you hear.

DAY 9

WHAT NOT TO DO

discover

READ 1 SAMUEL 28.

"The Lord has done exactly what he said through
me: The Lord has torn the kingship out of your
hand and given it to your neighbor David."
— 1 Samuel 28:17

David had been waiting patiently for God to open the door for his opportunity to be king. Saul had turned his back on God many years before (see 1 Samuel 15) and as David's strength and power rose, Saul's plummeted.

In today's verses, Saul was looking at certain defeat at the hands of the Philistines. To make matters worse for the Israelite king, David was fighting against Saul on behalf of the Philistines. Saul had nowhere to turn, so he sought out a medium (even though he had driven all the mediums out of his own land) to call up Samuel from the grave and give him advice—a practice that was strictly forbidden by God's law.

This woman, called a "witch" in some translations, was leading people away from seeking the Lord. Yet God, almighty in every situation, allowed Saul to see a vision of Samuel, hear truth, and realize his own sin.

The saddest part of this chapter is that Saul never repented; he knew he had turned his back on God and he knew he was living in unbelief, but he simply would not return to God. Not even the voice of the dead prophet could turn his heart and mind back. Saul's lack of faith cost him his kingdom, his sanity, and his life.

delight

Why didn't the Lord answer Saul's prayer (see v. 6)?

How do Saul's actions and attitude reflect his hope (or lack of it)?

display

Saul had turned his back on God, had sought to kill David (God's chosen successor), and had broken his own standards of not seeking the counsel of mediums. Like Saul, you may find yourself so far from God today that you can't imagine ever returning to your faith and His presence. But Saul's story doesn't need to be yours; God doesn't want anyone to perish, but desires for us all to come to repentance (see 2 Peter 3:9). Take time today to consider any words, actions, and attitudes you've had lately that reveal a lack of faith. Confess them to God and receive His forgiveness.

As you pray today, consider the ongoing acts of faith that God has called you to: prayer, forgiveness, worship, Bible reading, and sharing. Ask God to let you know where you've chosen to turn your back on these practices and consider how you can regularly make them part of your daily walk.

HONOR THE KING

discover

READ 2 SAMUEL 1.

**They mourned, wept, and fasted until the evening
for those who died by the sword—for Saul, his son
Jonathan, the Lord's people, and the house of Israel.
— 2 Samuel 1:12**

Most epic stories have a battle between good and evil; when good triumphs over evil, everyone celebrates. However, God's kingdom operates a little differently: in today's passage, when David's enemy (Saul) was killed on the battlefield, David mourned. What gives?

We can't forget the history these two men shared: David had been in the service of Saul since he had been a teenager, as a harp player and Saul's armor-bearer. After David had killed Goliath, he had served Saul for years faithfully, leading Saul's army into battle. He had even married Saul's daughter Michal.

Though their relationship soured, David always showed Saul honor: he didn't kill the king when he had a chance, didn't confront him in battle, and wouldn't let his men bring harm to Saul. David respected Saul and respected that he was God's chosen king for a time.

David's mourning wasn't obligatory or formal; he tore his clothes, mourned, wept, and fasted for Saul and Jonathan by his own choice. He led his men to do the same, and he led them in a song of lament for King Saul. The honor David showed Saul in life as well as in death revealed his reverence for God's plan and patience for His timing.

delight

What ultimately fueled David's reverence for Saul? What can you learn from this practice?

How can you better respect the people God has placed in authority over you at this stage in your life?

display

As we have seen in David's life so far, relationships are complicated. You can love someone and wish they lived 1000 miles away; you can miss someone and hope you never see them again. You can have an enemy and fondly remember the days when you were friends. In the space below or in a journal, jot down the names of five people with whom you have a complicated relationship. Next to each name, write two ways you can honor them this week. Some suggestions for honoring might include speaking positively about them to others, praying for them, sending them an encouraging message, or simply giving them a genuine smile.

As you pray today, consider a time you lost someone, either because they moved, they died, or some other situation in which you had to say goodbye. Pour out your regrets, emotion, and uncertainty to the Lord, entrusting Him with your heart, thoughts, and memories.

DAVID'S REIGN

SECTION 2

We covered the first part of David's life in only ten days of devotions. Though you explored those chapters quickly, don't let them fool you: fifteen years passed between the time David was anointed and the time Saul died. Though David probably thought his time had finally come, his struggles were far from over.

BROTHER AGAINST BROTHER

discover

READ 2 SAMUEL 2.

"Now, may the LORD show kindness and faithfulness to you, and I will also show the same goodness to you because you have done this deed. Therefore, be strong and valiant, for though Saul your lord is dead, the house of Judah has anointed me king over them."
— 2 Samuel 2:6-7

Saul was dead, as was his son Jonathan. David, after waiting so long to be king, was installed as the leader of Judah. But Judah was only the southern portion of Israel. Saul's commander, Abner, had placed Saul's son Ish-bosheth as the ruler of the northern part of Israel. As a result of these two kings grasping for leadership of a kingdom, a civil war ensued.

The division between these two territories was unnatural; they were all descendants of Abraham, God's chosen people. So when they begin to fight among themselves in today's reading, we might ask, "What in the world is going on? Why are they fighting?"

Great questions. Notice that the two rulers, David and Ish-bosheth, were not at the meeting of the armies. What had started out as two groups grasping for power turned into a bloody battle. Though on that day it seemed that David's men won, in reality, everybody lost. Foolish pride had turned what should have been a brotherhood into enemies.

delight

At the heart of this struggle was pride. When has pride—or unreasonable stubbornness—in your own heart caused you pain, struggle, or hardship?

Have you ever had tension or disunity in your own family? What was the cause of it? How was it resolved? What role do you play in these situations?

display

Though the people of Israel were divided between two kings, they should never have let politics invade their relationships. However, as the men jostled for position and glory, they turned on their own people— God's people. We do the same: sometimes the people that are closest to us become our fiercest enemies. So, we must be aware of tension and conflict in our relationships, seeking to end hard feelings before they drive a deeper wedge. Work on that over the coming week: do or say something kind to a friend or family member on each of the next seven days.

As you pray today, consider the conflicts you have with people in your life who should be your supporters: friends, close family, church leaders, or extended family. Do you consider any of these to be an enemy? Ask God to help you achieve restoration in that relationship, and invite Him to show you how you can take the first step toward love, healing, and forgiveness.

FRIEND? ENEMY? FRENEMY?

discover

READ 2 SAMUEL 3.

**Abner conferred with the elders of Israel: "In the past you
wanted David to be king over you. Now take action, because
the LORD has spoken concerning David: 'Through my
servant David I will save my people Israel from the power
of the Philistines and the power of all Israel's enemies.'"
— 2 Samuel 3:17-18**

As you read in today's chapter, the line between friend and enemy
gets blurred when feelings are hurt and dishonor enters a relationship.
David was gaining strength as Saul's son Ish-bosheth was losing
his. Apparently, the stress was getting to Ish-bosheth, and he falsely
accused Abner, his commander (as well as his father's commander
before him) of an immoral act. Abner was so insulted that he switched
loyalties to David and made it his goal to put David on the throne over
all of Israel.

Although Abner had chosen to support David, bad blood still existed
between Abner and Joab, David's commander, because Abner had
killed Joab's brother in battle (see 2 Sam. 2:18-23). When Joab found
himself close enough to Abner to kill him, he did it.

David was innocent in the murder, but he didn't distance himself from
Joab. Even as he recognized Abner's leadership, he realized the danger
Joab's hot-headed actions could put them in (see v. 39). Though David
was God's choice for king, he would need to learn to take charge of the
people around him. Quickly.

delight

How do you navigate relationships with people in your life who have hot tempers?

Think of friendship like a series of circles inside one another. In your inner circle should be people who bring you up and closer to God. Who is in your inner circle? Do they bring you up and closer to God?

display

We can talk all we want about who we follow, but our actions are what reveal our true hearts. In today's reading, Joab revealed through his actions that he didn't support David as king: he didn't listen to David and he didn't support David's decisions. In the space below, or in a journal, write about how well you honor the people you claim to support: God, parents, authorities, and friends. What do your actions reveal about your heart? You may need to go to one or more people and apologize for your attitude and actions toward them, then re-commit to honoring others.

God instructs us to submit to certain people because of the authority they have over us. As you pray today, consider those people in authority over you and pray for them. Pray that God would give them wisdom, patience, and love. Consider how David showed respect to Abner even in death.

The Shepherd King

STILL WAITING

discover

READ 2 SAMUEL 4.

"How much more when wicked men kill a righteous man in his own house on his own bed! So now, should I not require his blood from you and purge you from the earth?"
— 2 Samuel 4:11

David lived around 1000 BC—a brutal time period. If we had to summarize the lives of rulers at that time, it might be this: kill or be killed. You've already read about the death of Saul, Jonathan, and Abner; today we add Ish-bosheth to the list. It was a rough time to be in line for the throne!

In today's reading, we see that two brothers, Baanah and Rechab, took Ish-bosheth's life because they thought it would bring them favor with David. Betrayal, again, was their fiercest weapon. Ish-bosheth had trusted them as leaders of raiding parties, but they deceived him by walking into his house and murdering him in his bed!

David was furious: this was not the will of God. Yes, he had waited years and years to secure the throne. Yes, he had enemies. But God had put David on the particular life path of waiting patiently for God to open the door to being king, rather than using his own fighting ability or his mighty warriors. David didn't want the easy path to the throne—he wanted God's path.

delight

We will learn more about Mephibosheth later. Who is he? What do we know about him so far? (See verse 4.) Why might David care about what happens to him?

Baanah and Rechab expected praise for their actions against Ish-bosheth, but they received death instead. When was a time you did something for the wrong reason and got an unexpected outcome?

display

Sometimes, the hardest thing about waiting on God is entrusting Him to handle the situation. We get antsy, and we want to take matters into our own hands. Sometimes we choose to bypass living by faith, and instead we justify lying, hatred, immorality, greed, or dishonoring our parents in order to skip the hard part of living in obedience. But we can be certain that God's plan for our lives will never lead us down the path of sin. Are you skipping the hard work of perseverance and patience in some area of your life? Are you justifying sinful actions to get what you want? Take a moment and examine your heart. If the answer is "yes," repent and ask God to help you be patient and content with what He gives you.

Fortunately for us, God gives us the Holy Spirit, who leads us into repentance, holiness, and obedience. As you pray today, reflect on the words of John 14:26 and invite the Spirit to dwell in you with power and holiness. Recommit to walking His path for you.

PERFECT TIMING?

discover

READ 2 SAMUEL 5.

"Even while Saul was king over us, you were the one who led us out to battle and brought us back. The LORD also said to you, 'You will shepherd my people Israel, and you will be ruler over Israel.'" So all the elders of Israel came to the king at Hebron. King David made a covenant with them at Hebron in the Lord's presence, and they anointed David king over Israel.
— 2 Samuel 5:2-3

The best things come to those who wait. This is a familiar saying to us, and maybe there was a saying like it in David's day. But the biblical version sounds like this: "God's timing is best." David had sure learned patience as he waited for God's timing to be king!

It had been over twenty years since God sent Samuel to anoint David. Twenty years! During that time, David didn't kill Saul in order to be king, didn't kill his son Ish-bosheth to be king, and didn't force the citizens to accept him. As he patiently waited, the people finally came to David and asked him to rule over them. And with his first act—taking back Jerusalem—David showed the power of the Lord and the reward to those who wait for Him.

David made Jerusalem his capital city, where he gained power, made friends with other kings, and found confidence in God's place for him on the throne of Israel. Was it worth waiting twenty years? David would say "Yes!"

delight

What are three ways in this chapter that David demonstrated he trusted God's plan?

How has God given you confidence for where He has brought you in life?

display

Verse 12 in today's passage gives us insight into David's heart and mind during his years of waiting to be king over all Israel: it wasn't until it actually happened that he really knew that God had established him to be king. That tells us that during the years of waiting, David wasn't 100% sure. He had questions, setbacks, and struggles. You will, too, but that doesn't mean God's plan isn't in progress. Today, in the space below, or in a journal, write about your own doubts and fears in the presence of the Lord. Never forget, He desires what is best for you and will give you what you need when you need it.

As you pray today, find courage in taking your fears to God; He is mightier than anything that may make you fearful! With the God of Armies on your side, you will find your purpose and your calling within your faith.

MEMORY VERSE

2 Samuel 7:8-9

"So now this is what you are to say to my servant David: 'This is what the LORD of Armies says: I took you from the pasture, from tending the flock, to be ruler over my people Israel. I have been with you wherever you have gone, and I have destroyed all your enemies before you. I will make a great name for you like that of the greatest on the earth.'"

DAVID'S HOLY MOVES

discover

READ 2 SAMUEL 6.

> David feared the LORD that day and said, "How can the
> ark of the LORD ever come to me?" So he was not willing
> to bring the ark of the LORD to the city of David; instead,
> he diverted it to the house of Obed-edom of Gath.
> — 2 Samuel 6:9-10

The ark of God (also called the ark of the covenant or the ark of the Lord) was a holy artifact that had accompanied the Israelites since the time they had followed Moses through the wilderness into the promised land. The ark represented the presence of God with His people on earth, and it had a prescribed place in the tabernacle. However, it had been captured by the Philistines before Saul had become king.

So, as one of his first acts as king over a united Israel, David decided to return the ark to its home in the tabernacle. Only there was a problem: David, and the priests whose responsibility it was to move the ark, hadn't looked back in the Law to see how they were supposed to transport it. The Philistines had used a cart pulled by oxen to carry it, so the Israelites followed this pattern. And because this wasn't God's plan, a man lost his life when the oxen stumbled.

When they tried the second time, David and the priests obeyed the Lord, worshiping and sacrificing the whole way. As they had learned the hard way, the only way to truly honor and respect the Lord is to walk in obedience. And that means knowing what His Word says.

delight

The ark was a sacred object for the Israelites. What are some sacred or important things in your life that require respect and care? How can you honor God with how you take care of these items?

David learned from his mistakes and adjusted his plans when he moved the ark a second time. When was a time you have learned from mistakes and changed your actions?

display

Sometimes we, like David, want to do great things for God without stopping long enough to consider God's instructions on how to honor Him. God loves it when we desire to bring Him glory, but He also expects His people to know His commands. We shouldn't just wait until we need specific advice to know what the Bible says; we must be seeking it daily, through reading, studying, memorizing, and meditating. What kind of Bible reading or study plan are you following? How devoted to it are you? Talk to your parents, youth pastor, small group leader, or a trusted spiritual mentor if you need help making a plan.

Open your Bible to Psalm 119 today; it's divided into sections, but the theme of each section is the same: the greatness of God's Word. Use one of those sections as your prayer today. Spend time telling God the glory of His Word and your commitment to knowing it, reading it, and following it.

WHOSE HOUSE IS THIS?

discover

READ 2 SAMUEL 7:1-17.

"So now this is what you are to say to my servant David: 'This is what the LORD of Armies says: I took you from the pasture, from tending the flock, to be ruler over my people Israel. I have been with you wherever you have gone, and I have destroyed all your enemies before you. I will make a great name for you like that of the greatest on the earth.... Your house and kingdom will endure before me forever, and your throne will be established forever.'"
— 2 Samuel 7:8-9,16

David had become king and had received many blessings in waiting on God's perfect timing. He couldn't take any credit for his rise to power—everything he had received had been given to him by God. In order to honor God for his success, David thought it might be a good idea to build God a permanent structure: a temple. Nathan, God's prophet, thought it sounded like a great idea, too. But that night, God came to Nathan and changed their plans; in all their good ideas, nobody had consulted Him.

Instead, God explained, David's son would build the temple, not David. Not only that, but God would build a spiritual house for David, one that would last forever. God had taken a noble idea—not in His plan, but still noble—and instead blessed David with a gift that would surpass any other. The loyal love of God would be part of David's son's life and the life of each of his descendants after that. No blessing from a human could ever approach such an amazing gift.

delight

Clearly David's heart was in the right place, but his plan wasn't God's plan. How can you know the difference between something that sounds like a good idea and something that God blesses and desires for you to do?

Using a Bible app or online Bible, look up 2 Samuel 7:8 in three different translations (such as the Christian Standard Bible [CSB], English Standard Version [ESV], and the New International Version [NIV]). In each translation, what is God called? What can you learn about God from these different translations of His name in this verse?

display

David's heart was turned toward God and His glory. But even a good idea isn't always in God's plans for us. That's why our relationship with the Lord is based in dwelling *with* Him rather than working *for* Him. It's great to start a prayer club at school, go on mission trips, and serve others in Jesus's name. But it must come from an overflow of our relationship with God through time in the Word, prayer, worship, and love. Take time to day to talk with God and hear His voice. Ask Him if anything you are currently doing for Him might not be something He wants you to do.

As you pray today, consider the activities you do regularly. Ask God, "Is this in Your plan for me at this time in my life?" Wait patiently— maybe days, maybe longer—to see if God redirects your heart or mind in that area.

The Shepherd King

WHO AM I?

discover

READ 2 SAMUEL 7:18-29.

Then King David went in, sat in the Lord's presence, and said, "Who am I, Lord God, and what is my house that you have brought me this far?"
— 2 Samuel 7:18

In yesterday's verses, God promised David that He would build a lasting legacy, a spiritual house, for David's ancestors forever. Though we understand that God was pointing to Jesus—who would come from the lineage of David—we don't know if David grasped all the significance of God's blessing on his family.

However, David understood enough to know that this blessing was astronomical. His response was to go to the tabernacle, into the presence of the Lord, and ask, "Who am I?" Who was he to deserve such a lavish blessing? David's prayer is one of utter and complete thanksgiving and humility. Throughout history when God's people have encountered Him by hearing His voice, grasping His Word, or receiving His blessings, deep humility and praise is the result. David was no different.

David acknowledged the blessing of God's promise: it wasn't just for him, but for all humanity, now and forever. Only the Lord of Armies could make such a powerful promise and guarantee it would come to pass. God's power, plan, and presence are "great and awesome" (v. 23) and David gave God credit for His people standing out from all others.

David ended his prayer with confident words: God would fulfill His promise. He was the Lord of Armies, and His words were true. David was confident in God because he knew God and trusted Him.

delight

What words or phrases that David used to describe God in these verses stand out to you? Why?

When you've had an encounter with God—great or small—what has been your reaction?

display

David's response to God was one of utter humility: God is holy, all-powerful, and perfect. He sat in the Lord's presence (see v. 18), humbling himself as he acknowledged his amazing Lord. We, like David, will sometimes find ourselves overwhelmed by an awareness of God: perhaps in reading His Word, experiencing true worship, or realizing His faithfulness to us as He acts in our lives. Our attitude should be the same as David's was: complete thanksgiving and humility. Take some time today and find a place where you can sit in the Lord's presence, thank Him aloud for His blessing in your life, and speak aloud your confidence in His promises.

Make your prayer today one of thanksgiving. Thank Him for your blessings, thank Him for who He is, and thank Him for His promises. Then allow yourself to dig even deeper: thank Him for your trials, your difficulties, and your struggles. Believe that He has a perfect plan and will carry it through to completion.

DAY 18

UNCHANGED

discover

READ 2 SAMUEL 8.

**So David reigned over all Israel, administering
justice and righteousness for all his people.
— 2 Samuel 8:15**

David waited decades for God to allow him to finally sit on the throne of Israel. As you've followed along with David's story, have you caught yourself waiting for him to change for the worse once he became king? Honestly, so often in the Bible (or in history or in life) there are some pretty awesome people who seem to let power and victory go to their heads. We've seen David stay committed and focused on God when he was in the middle of struggle, but how about once he reached the pinnacle?

Until this point, we see great things in David: none of his victories turned him away from the Lord or made him overconfident. He was dealing with the struggles and battles of an entire nation; yet, in his fighting, he was still able to listen to God and follow Him.

David reigned over Israel with justice and righteousness. Sometimes we read passages like today's and think, "But David was so brutal!" In our world, that may seem to be the case. But God had called David to make Israel into a victorious, prosperous, God-glorifying nation in a world that was very different than ours is today. However, pay attention to how David showed mercy, even as he conquered other nations: he spared lives, he gave what was gained through war to the Lord, and as new people entered his kingdom, he treated them with justice and righteousness. Success didn't change David!

delight

Has success ever gone to your head? What happened? How did you come back down to earth?

David had a reputation among the nations that surrounded Israel. What is your reputation? Does it bring glory to God? If not, how can you change it to be one that honors Him?

display

Like David, we all experience the different seasons of life: waiting, struggle, hope, victory. Regardless of the season you're in right now, your calling is still the same as David's: be faithful to the Lord. He makes us patient in our waiting, stronger in our struggles, joyful in our hope, and God-glorifying in our victory. Today, consider the season of your own life: Which one are you in? Then consider if your faith has changed in this season: Are you bitter, impatient, prideful, or boasting? As you see your own heart and mind clearly, be sure your calling and faith don't waver through the different seasons but instead remain focused on Him.

As you pray today, thank God for your victories. They may be big, like, "Lord! Thank you for giving me the chance to share a story from the Bible today!" Or, they may be somewhat small, such as, "Lord! I didn't lose my cool when someone made me mad!" God gives you victories; thank Him for them.

ME-PHIB-O-WHO?

discover

READ 2 SAMUEL 9.

**David asked, "Is there anyone remaining from the family
of Saul I can show kindness to for Jonathan's sake?"
— 2 Samuel 9:1**

The accolades and blessings had been piling up for David: he was king over the united kingdom, he had been victorious in battle, and the Lord had guided him through each struggle and trial. But we see here that David hadn't forgotten his past: he still remembered his friend Jonathan, the son of Saul, who had been killed in battle.

Not satisfied to simply remember Jonathan, David went out of his way to find anyone in Saul's family who was still alive. Upon finding one of Saul's old servants, Ziba, he discovered that Jonathan's son, Mephibosheth (pronounced *meh-FIB-oh-sheth*), wasn't that far away.

Mephibosheth was mentioned briefly in 2 Samuel 4:4 (on Day 13), where it was explained that when he was about five years old, his nanny had picked him up to flee after hearing that Saul and Jonathan had been killed. The nanny had been in such a hurry that she had dropped Mephibosheth, injuring his feet, and he hadn't walked properly since.

When he was summoned by David, he was probably fearful; many kings killed any living relatives of an old regime. Imagine his surprise, then, when David did the opposite: he invited Mephibosheth to come live in the palace! Not only that, but David gave Mephibosheth all of Saul's land and appointed Ziba, as well as Ziba's entire family, to be servants for him.

delight

Why do you think David wanted to show kindness to someone from the family of his old enemy? How can that challenge us to consider who we show kindness to in our lives?

How does David's kindness toward Mephibosheth reveal what was in his heart?

display

David was king over all Israel, but he still reached down to the lowliest: grandson of the former king, hidden and forgotten, disabled, not even living in his own house. Of all David's mighty acts, this one may have been the one that best displayed his heart: for no reason, he chose to bring Mephibosheth into his family. God does the same for us: out of His great love for us, He saved us and called us His children. We, too, are called to be kind and compassionate, full of grace and encouragement. Who needs your encouraging words, kind touch, or smile today?

As you pray today, consider all the wonderful things God has done for you. Did you have breakfast this morning? Do you have a place to call home? Do you have a pet or a friend that makes you laugh? Don't forget that God is the source of all help and joy. Thank Him for those blessings and the blessings yet to come in your life.

DAY 20

PICK YOUR BATTLE

discover

READ 2 SAMUEL 10.

Then David said, "I'll show kindness to Hanun son of Nahash, just as his father showed kindness to me." So David sent his emissaries to console Hanun concerning his father. However, when they arrived in the land of the Ammonites, the Ammonite leaders said to Hanun their lord, "Just because David has sent men with condolences for you, do you really believe he's showing respect for your father? Instead, hasn't David sent his emissaries in order to scout out the city, spy on it, and demolish it?"
— 2 Samuel 10:2-3

David had been successful in battle, and he had made political allies along the way; the king of the Ammonites was one of them. When that king died, David sent messengers to convey his condolences. But the Ammonite leaders were suspicious of David's motives: Was he really being kind, or was he sending men to spy on their city? They decided to believe the second.

So they disrespected the messengers, mistreating and humiliating them. David responded with action, planning a complex battle strategy that defeated the Ammonites and made it clear that the humiliation of his men, who he had sent out of compassion, would not be tolerated.

David had sought peace and kindness in this situation, but had received mistreatment in return. He knew that his enemies weren't only mistreating his men, but were ridiculing his God, as well. David wasn't afraid to stand up for his God, his nation, and his army.

The Shepherd King

delight

Look carefully at David's words in verse 2. What was his motivation for sending the messengers?

It can be easy to think this story gives you the right to take revenge on people who humiliate you. Seek the full counsel of the Bible before you believe that—verses such as Matthew 5:39 give the full picture. Instead, consider this a story of righting a wrong and seeking justice. Where can you stand up for what is right in your life, in a non-vengeful way?

display

David's experience can sometimes be our own: there are times when people simply mistreat us. Even if we didn't do anything wrong and even if our motives were pure, sometimes others will be cruel. Sometimes, people are cruel to us simply because we follow Jesus and stand for righteousness. Like David, we should never be people who instigate trouble or treat others poorly. However, we sometimes need to be prepared to take a stand for ourselves, our family, our friends, and our faith. What would be a good way to respond to someone's unkind words or actions? Write about it below.

As you pray today, ask God to examine your heart and mind: Are your words kind? Are your motives pure? Are your actions reflecting God's instructions? Read through 1 Peter 3:13-16, remembering that even if you suffer for your good actions, you can still be gentle and reverent, keeping a clear conscience.

The Shepherd King

DAVID'S REGRET AND REDEMPTION

If the story of David's life ended after 2 Samuel 10, we'd remember him as nothing but a hero. Unfortunately, all heroes have a weakness, and David's was the same as yours and everyone else's: sin. Though David had a heart that sought after God, he still let his sinful desires lead him down paths God would never want him to walk.

DAVID'S REGRET

discover

READ 2 SAMUEL 11.

**One evening David got up from his bed and strolled around
on the roof of the palace. From the roof he saw a woman
bathing—a very beautiful woman. So David sent someone
to inquire about her, and he said, "Isn't this Bathsheba,
daughter of Eliam and wife of Uriah the Hethite?"
— 2 Samuel 11:2-3**

If there ever were a chance for a re-do, David would have liked to have one in this chapter of his life. By the end of 2 Samuel 11, David was a murderer and an adulterer, and "the LORD considered what David had done to be evil" (v. 27). But David's horrible sin didn't start with murder; it started in the gray area: "In the spring when kings march out to war, David sent Joab . . ." (v. 1). This all started because David wasn't with his army, where he was supposed to be.

Next, he was doing what he wasn't supposed to do: he saw something he wanted and took it, even though it—she!—wasn't his to have. This quickly escalated from simply looking lustfully, to coveting, and then to adultery. At this stage we don't get any explanation that David was repentant over his sin; tragically, we only see that he tried to cover it up.

Finally, a deceitful plan to trick Bathsheba's husband led to an honorable and innocent man's death. Though the story seems over, God hadn't stepped into it yet. That will be revealed tomorrow.

delight

At what point do you think David should have been aware of his sin? How did the person he sent to inquire about Bathsheba try to dissuade him from sin?

In what ways did David deceive himself in this story?

display

Re-read 2 Samuel 11, and as you do, consider how many of the Ten Commandments David broke in this short period of time (see Ex. 20:1-17 or Deut. 5:6-21 to review these commandments). Write these violations in the space below as you read. Then carefully consider: What are you doing when you face temptation in your own life? Do you, like David, ignore the warnings and simply do what you want? Are you carefully guarding what you see, hear, and think? What lies are you believing about your actions? God is not okay with sin. How is He helping you fight temptation and avoid sin today? Write these answers below, as well.

Pour your heart out before the Lord, confessing your known sins and your willful disobedience. Then read 2 Corinthians 11:2-3 and ask God to reveal to you where you have been deceived by the enemy. Consider how you can keep your mind, eyes, heart, emotions, and actions purely focused on the Lord.

DAY 22

"YOU ARE THE MAN!"

discover

READ 2 SAMUEL 12.

David responded to Nathan, "I have sinned against the LORD." Then Nathan replied to David, "And the LORD has taken away your sin; you will not die."
— 2 Samuel 12:13

David's sin in 2 Samuel 11 comes to light in today's chapter. The prophet Nathan, who you previously read about in 2 Samuel 7, found out what David had done. He may have heard from someone in the palace; after all, David's affair and plot was hardly a secret. Or Nathan may have heard directly from the Lord; he was a prophet, after all.

Either way, Nathan confronted David with a story. Nathan's story mirrored David's horrifying deed, and David responded with righteous fury. Nathan used this emotional response to drive home his holy point: David was the guilty party. David had everything he had ever dreamed of, with more still to come, and still he had stolen another man's wife—then murdered her husband!—simply because he wanted her. His cover-up and sins were never hidden from God.

From here on, because of David's sin, his family would always be entrenched in bloody conflict. On top of that, the son born to Bathsheba would die. However, when he was confronted with his sin, David was convicted and his heart was broken before God. He did all the things he should have done: he confessed his sins, genuinely repented, and humbled himself before the Lord. David was forgiven, but the lasting consequences of his sin lingered. This event marked the turning point in David's family, reign, and faith.

delight

Why do you think God instructed Nathan to confront David with this parable instead of just calling him out for his sin?

How did God show mercy in the midst of punishing David's sin?

display

What a sad, horrible ending to a story that never needed to happen. Sin is avoidable because God is faithful to always provide a way out of each and every temptation (see 1 Cor. 10:13). But when the temptation triumphs, our sin hurts our relationship with God. We already read Psalm 51 on Day 1, but read it again, knowing that David wrote it after Nathan confronted him. If you come across any phrase that applies to sin in your own life, speak those words aloud, using David's words to lead you in your confession.

Hopefully, you've added regular confession to your daily prayer. The ongoing cleansing from sin is healthy for your faith and keeps your relationship with God clean. Today, add a prayer that God would allow you to see temptation clearly and that you would trust Him as you walk away from it.

The Shepherd King

DISASTER

discover

READ 2 SAMUEL 13.

(Warning: this is a terrible story that deals with sexual trauma.)

**After Absalom had fled to Geshur and had been there
three years, King David longed to go to Absalom, for
David had finished grieving over Amnon's death.
— 2 Samuel 13:38-39**

Honestly, this story is hard to read because it reveals the worst of humanity. David had many children by different wives (see 1 Chron. 3:1-9). Absalom and Tamar were brother and sister from the same mother; Amnon was a half-brother to them. Amnon lusted after his half-sister Tamar and made an evil plan to lure her into his bedroom, where he sexually assaulted her.

Tamar suffered immeasurably for Amnon's horrific act. Not only did she experience the brutality of the sexual assault, but she was shamed by Amnon's actions and "lived as a desolate woman in the house of her brother Absalom" (v. 20). Suffice it to say: her life was never the same after this.

Absalom was immediately furious and hated Amnon. His response was to devise a plan to have his men murder Amnon because of what he had done to his sister.

One frustratingly missing part of this already terrible story is David—though he heard about Amnon's horrible act again Tamar and was "furious" (v. 21), he didn't do anything. Sin piled upon sin, and this family was being ripped apart.

delight

Why do you think David didn't do anything in this situation?

Verse 15 is hard to read but reveals an important truth: sin is never satisfying. It only brings about hatred of others and ultimately ourselves. How can you remind yourself of this truth as a means to flee from temptation when it arises?

display

One of the craziest aspects of this story hits us when we remember who all the players are: David's children! The same David who defeated Goliath, waited patiently for the throne, and wanted to build a temple for God had children who could set out to rape and murder. Their horrible acts were atrocious, but it is a strong reminder to each of us that our faith doesn't come from our parents; we must choose to follow the Lord on our own! What are you doing today to strengthen your faith and make it your own? Write a few ideas below or in a journal.

As you pray today, ask God to give you the proper perspective when someone around you sins. If you have influence in their life, speak truth and righteousness in love. If you have access to help someone who is hurting, be compassionate and advocate for the victim. If you have been wronged, ask God to give you grace to forgive, hope for the future, and to help you find your strength and identity in Him.

TRICKED AND TRICKY

discover

READ 2 SAMUEL 14.

**Joab went to the king and told him. So David summoned
Absalom, who came to the king and paid homage with his face
to the ground before him. Then the king kissed Absalom.**
— 2 Samuel 14:33

Today's passage shows the fallout from yesterday's horrific story.
Absalom fled to Geshur, around 100 miles away, because David
was furious with him. After three years, David's anger had subsided
(see 2 Sam. 13:38-39) but Absalom was still living in isolation from
his family. Joab, David's general, realized that the king was distracted
by the separation from his son and enlisted a woman to come before
David, pretending to have a son who killed the other and asking David
for mercy.

Joab's trick worked. David's verdict revealed that he was willing to grant
mercy to a stranger's murderous son but hadn't granted mercy to his
own. He saw his own hard-hardheartedness and relented in letting
Absalom return to Jerusalem. However, David didn't open his arms
wide for the returning son; his requirement was that Absalom not enter
his sight.

Absalom lived out of sight in Jerusalem for two years, and no one
would give him an audience. When he burned Joab's field, that finally
got David's attention. Father and son were reunited, but with an
obvious tension. The story continues tomorrow.

The Shepherd King

delight

How might you describe David's heart in this passage, considering his words and actions?

When someone hurts us, forgiveness is necessary, but so are boundaries. How can you put up healthy boundaries around those who have hurt you in the past, while also learning to genuinely forgive them in your heart?

display

On the surface, this seems to be a story about forgiveness. But forgiveness shouldn't feel forced and fake, as David's and Absalom's truce seems to be. The forgiveness we receive from God is full and based in His love. The blood of Jesus was poured out for the forgiveness of our sins (see Matt. 26:28). When we come to God in repentance and humility, we can receive His forgiveness and restoration. Take time today to praise God for forgiving you of your sin, your selfishness, your bad attitudes, and your pride. Write your praise in the space below or in a journal, and consider adding additional prayers of praise as they come to you throughout the rest of this year.

Before praying today, read Matthew 5:21-26. Consider if you have any issues with a brother or sister (or friend, or family member, or teacher, or anyone else) and need to offer forgiveness. Ask God to show you whether your forgiveness is genuine or superficial.

MEMORY VERSE

2 SAMUEL 22:2-3

He said:
"The Lord is my rock,
my fortress,
and my deliverer,
my God, my rock
where I seek refuge.
My shield, the horn
of my salvation,
my stronghold,
my refuge, and my Savior,
you save me from violence."

FAMILY CHAOS

discover

READ 2 SAMUEL 15.

"However, if he should say, 'I do not delight in you,' then here I am—he can do with me whatever pleases him."
— 2 Samuel 15:26

This battle had been brewing for years, and in today's reading, the feud between David and his son Absalom became an all-out war. Absalom spent years gaining a following among the people of Israel by promising that he would be a better ruler than his father. He portrayed an image of power and fairness, and he "stole the hearts of the men of Israel" (v. 6).

Absalom then pretended to go to Hebron to worship, when in reality he was headed there to proclaim that he was king. Others he had invited got caught up in the conspiracy, and with the addition of one of David's advisors, Absalom's coup was underway.

David realized he'd been unseated by his son and left the palace with his family and closest allies. They fled on foot, adding allies as they went. David sent back his priest Zadok and personal adviser, Hushai, in an attempt to confuse or mislead Absalom.

David sent the ark back to Jerusalem, as well. It had always accompanied David and his men into battle, reminding them that the Lord was fighting for them. In this instance, though, David wasn't sure: Was he doing the right thing? Should Absalom be king? What he did know, however, was that the ark belonged in Jerusalem. As he fled, he trusted that God was still sovereign and His will would be done in this situation.

delight

You may be able to relate to having a family in chaos (hopefully not to this extreme, though). How can you be an agent of peace within your family dynamic?

In verse 26, David displayed his ultimate faith in God, trusting that if God desired for him to return to Jerusalem, He would make it happen. How can you place your ultimate faith in God regardless of your circumstances?

display

The tentative, half-hearted offer of forgiveness that David gave to Absalom in chapter 14 became the start of Absalom's sneaky, manipulative play for the throne. You've probably found yourself in David's position: on the receiving end of cruelty, hatred, or deception. It hurts deeply, especially if the person attacking you was a friend or family member. But we, like David, must remember that God is still in control, even when we feel like our life is out of control. To help, think of a worship song that reminds you of God's power and love; listen to it and keep it playing in your mind and heart today.

As you pray today, follow Jesus's instruction to love your enemies and pray for them (see Matt. 5:44). Pour out your heart to God, confessing any unkind words and unholy thoughts you may be holding on to. Ask for God to fill you with His love and compassion in every situation.

BITTERSWEET VICTORY

discover

READ 2 SAMUEL 18.

Absalom was riding on his mule when he happened to meet David's soldiers. When the mule went under the tangled branches of a large oak tree, Absalom's head was caught fast in the tree. The mule under him kept going, so he was suspended in midair.
— 2 Samuel 18:9

David and the people loyal to him had fled, but that wasn't the end of the story. In 2 Samuel 16–17, Absalom conspired with his advisors as to the best way to defeat his father, once and for all. But David had spies listening in on their conversations, and he was ready for Absalom's attack.

The troops were arranged and sent out to fight Absalom, with the very specific instruction: do not harm Absalom. Yes, he had betrayed his father, but David still loved him and didn't want him dead. Unfortunately for David and Absalom, Joab didn't agree with David's edict and didn't follow it. When he saw Absalom caught in a tree by the hair, he personally oversaw the young man's execution.

Joab did what he thought was best and ignored David's instructions. In doing so, he broke David's heart. Though Absalom's revolt had come to an end, David's victory was overshadowed by the death of his son. David had tasted the victory provided by the Lord, but he also knew the pain of death and the continued tragedy his sin left behind.

delight

Would you consider Joab to be a good friend to David? How can you learn from David's choices in friendship?

Do you think it was right for David not to celebrate his army's victory? Why do you feel this way?

display

Some situations are good (your favorite ice cream for dessert) and some are bad (getting stung by a wasp). But many situations are both good and bad, like if making a team you tried out for means giving up another activity you enjoy. David was in a similar situation: his men had won the battle, but he had lost his son in the process. Sometimes, like David, we love a person even though they treat us poorly or make bad choices. Only God's compassion and mercy can guide us through those situations with mixed emotions. If you have a complicated relationship in your life like David did, spend some time in prayer seeking God's direction for how you should handle this situation. Also, don't forget to consult God's Word for encouragement and direction.

What situation has you confused? Spend time talking through that situation with God. Tell him if you struggle to love someone in your family or if someone who claims to be your friend is treating you badly. God can handle your hard times and your conflicted emotions, and He wants to give you direction.

DAVID'S RESTORATION

discover

READ 2 SAMUEL 19.

**So he won over all the men of Judah, and they unanimously
sent word to the king: "Come back, you and all your servants."
— 2 Samuel 19:14**

Sometimes it's easy to forget that Bible stories happened in a real place and in a real time. Today we read that the issues surrounding Absalom's attempt to overthrow his father David had spiritual and historic implications, as well as a lasting political effect. When Absalom had unseated David, some of the people of Israel had taken sides, either joining "team Absalom" or remaining loyal to "team David." When Absalom was killed, however, the nation fractured into alliances.

Joab saw the struggle for allegiance of the nation and gave David wise advice: if David kept mourning over Absalom and forgot the people of his nation, he would lose his throne. So David restored not only his place as king over all of Israel but also renewed some friendships that had been strained as he left Jerusalem.

It had been a hard time for David, and not everyone agreed with his decisions and actions. Some of the decisions David made weren't the wisest or godliest. But eventually he was won over by wise counsel and he continued to seek God's voice among all the other opinions around him. On his journey back to Jerusalem, he stopped cowering and began acting like a king again. Even in the midst of human conflict, we must seek and hear God's direction.

delight

In verse 13 David replaced his commander Joab. Sometimes there are relationships in our lives that need to be removed. How do you know when to change the nature of—or even end—a relationship with someone?

How did David mend some of his relationships that had been torn or broken over the years?

The Shepherd King

display

It's impossible to please everyone. If you've ever tried to help two friends get along when they don't want to, you've experienced the struggle. We cannot tie our happiness, our identity, or our actions to people; we'll undoubtedly make them mad or let them down at some point, and they'll inevitably do the same for us. Instead, we must consider what it takes to please God. He alone gives us identity, peace, and direction. Today, go to a quiet place. Calm your heart and mind, and then read Romans 12:18. Say to God, "Lord, as far as I can help it, let me live in peace with others." Let God's Word shape who you are and how to live today.

It's tricky to navigate friendships and family with grace, love, and peace. If we try to handle them in our own power, we're sure to fail. Today, pray that God would give you guidance in your relationships. Surrender your attempts to control others, and give God the authority He deserves over your relationships.

WHY I SING

discover

READ 2 SAMUEL 22.

He said: "The LORD is my rock, my fortress, and my
deliverer, my God, my rock where I seek refuge. My
shield, the horn of my salvation, my stronghold, my
refuge, and my Savior, you save me from violence."
— 2 Samuel 22:2-3

David wrote many songs; they are recorded in the book of Psalms. This
chapter is also a song, written "on the day the LORD rescued [David]
from the grasp of all his enemies and from the grasp of Saul" (v. 1). We
don't know what day this was exactly, but we know it was in a period of
calm in David's life.

King David had turned to God to save him in many battles and
struggles, and we can see the warlike imagery in these verses. David
calls God his rock, fortresses, shield, and stronghold, and gives God
credit for his every victory. God had saved David from his enemies and
from the waves of death, and rescued him time and again.

David credits God's way for being "perfect" and His Word for being
"pure" (v. 31). It's only because David followed the guidance of God that
he found success in anything. God's leadership gave David victory. In
following God, he found success, triumph, and confidence. In addition,
we see the relationship between God and David: David cried out, and
God heard, answered, and acted.

delight

How many times does David use the word "my" to describe God in this chapter? What does this tell you?

In this song, David recounts how God protected and saved him over the years. When has God saved or protected you? Write about the first memory or memories that come to mind.

display

In a time of peace and reflection, David sat down and considered all that God had done in his life; these words are the song that flowed from his heart. Like David, we are wise to regularly take time and consider all that God has done in our lives. At some point today, sit down and write your own psalm of thanksgiving. Like David did, answer the following questions: Who is God to you? How has He been mighty in your life? How has He responded to your cries?

David's song is sometimes a conversation with God and sometimes a conversation to others about God. As you pray today, consider not only how you can converse with God about your struggles but also how you can testify to His faithfulness in the midst of your trial.

DAY 29

STOP COUNTING!

discover

READ 2 SAMUEL 24.

He built an altar to the LORD there and offered burnt offerings and fellowship offerings. Then the LORD was receptive to prayer for the land, and the plague on Israel ended.
— 2 Samuel 24:25

An alternate title to this chapter might be, "David's Last Big Mess." In the twenty-nine days that you've read about the life of King David, you've seen that it took decades for him to actually become king. In those days of struggle, he leaned heavily on the Lord and found success. But, when he got comfortable, David often stopped depending on God.

Today's chapter reveals what happens when we find our strength and confidence in something other than God: we realize that we have nothing without Him. David pridefully wanted to know how mighty his army was and took a census of the people, falling into Satan's temptation (see 1 Chron. 21:1). Taking a census wasn't normally a big deal, but the minute David heard the results, he realized his actions had been motivated by sin (see v. 10).

David confessed his sin, but God still saw punishment as necessary. Even in all His mercy, God will not make light of our sin. Because of David's pride, 70,000 people died in a plague. But just as the angel of death reached the edge of Jerusalem, God extended mercy. David bought that spot of land, offered a sacrifice, and the Lord stopped the plague.

delight

David didn't pay attention to the warnings he received before he initiated the census of the land. When have you not paid attention to a warning? What was the result?

Taking a census usually wouldn't have been a big deal—but in this case, David did it to see how awesome he was in his own eyes. God needed to remind David who he really needed to depend on. How do you remember to depend on God throughout your days?

display

David wasn't perfect; no one is. We know more about David and his sins than we do about many other people in the Bible. But we also see that, no matter what, he never turned his back on God. And God never turned His back on David. David constantly strove for obedience, and when he failed, he sought God for forgiveness and reconciliation. His sacrifice was great because he realized his own sinfulness. What might you sacrifice from your own life to clean out the things that tempt you to stray from your walk with God? Write your thoughts below.

As you pray today, carefully consider how your sins affect others. Ask God to guard your mind and heart from sin so that you can protect your relationship with Him and with others. If you see your own sin clearly, invite God to show you how you can mend the relationships that were hurt as a result.

THE KING'S FINAL WORDS

discover

READ 1 KINGS 2.

"...and keep your obligation to the LORD your God to walk in
his ways and to keep his statutes, commands, ordinances, and
decrees. This is written in the law of Moses, so that you will
have success in everything you do and wherever you turn."
— 1 Kings 2:3

As you might imagine, there was quite a family catastrophe as David
neared death. God had chosen Solomon as the next king, but Adonijah,
another of David's sons, was older and wanted the throne. Joab had
supported Adonijah, and it looked as though there would be a struggle
for who would be the ruler after David.

David was firm in his decision: it would be Solomon. The majority of
David's last instructions point Solomon to obey the Lord, keep the
written law, walk faithfully, and be whole-hearted in obedience.

David also gave Solomon some last-minute instructions for handling
some unfinished business: who should be punished, who should be
rewarded, and who should be watched carefully. Solomon listened to
the words of warning and care from David, doing almost exactly what
he was told.

And so we say goodbye to King David. His life is one that we look
to with respect: he sought the Lord, he found victory in following
the Lord, and he pointed others to the Lord. He wasn't perfect, but
when he failed, he faithfully turned back to God. Ultimately, the
greatest redemption for David came hundreds of years later, when his
descendant, Jesus, would give His life for the sins of the world and
pave a way for the whole world to be redeemed.

The Shepherd King

delight

What instructions from David's last words in this chapter sound like good instructions for you?

Can you imagine the shadow David cast that Solomon had to walk in? Maybe you feel like someone in your life casts a big shadow (like a parent, a sibling, or a spiritual mentor). How do you walk in faithfulness to God, creating your own legacy of faithfulness rather than feeling pressure to follow in someone else's footsteps?

display

When you follow God with all your heart, like David did, you walk in close fellowship with Him. Walking with God doesn't mean that everything will be great and go your way, but it means you trust Him to handle your battles, your struggles, and the situations where you don't know what to do. How closely are you walking with God today? Do you hear His voice? Are you obeying the things you know to obey? Take a quick walk around your neighborhood or a nearby park and invite God to join you; listen to what He has to say.

As you pray today, thank the Lord for the stories about David that are recorded in the Bible. Take a moment to consider all you have learned about God through the passages you've been exploring, and ask God how He would want you to live your life more—or less—like King David.

What's In Your Heart?

Our hearts are more important than we often like to think. Scripture calls them "the source of life" (Prov. 4:23). We're told to care for them, to guard them, to trust the Lord with everything we have in them (see Prov. 3:5-6). The Bible also says our hearts are liars, but that God gives us new hearts when we turn to Him for salvation (see Jer. 17:9; Ezek. 36:26).

While our world presses the heavy weight of appearances down on our shoulders, God looks at the heart. He calls to us with an invitation: "Take up my yoke and learn from me, because I am lowly and humble in heart, and you will find rest for your souls. For my yoke is easy and my burden is light" (Matt. 11:29-30).

Even after we trust in Jesus for salvation, we will still struggle. Our new hearts aren't immune to the world's charms or temptations. Even David, who was called a man after God's own heart (see 1 Sam 13:14; Acts 13:22) failed sometimes. His heart lied to him, too. And he cried out to God, "God, create a clean heart for me and renew a steadfast spirit within me" (Ps. 51:10).

Spend a few minutes reading the Scripture references on this page. Which one connected to your heart? Write it out below and focus on it.

Then, ask the Holy Spirit to examine your heart and show you if you, like David might need to ask God to cleanse your heart too. Write out anything that comes to mind as you feel led.

After having examined David's life for the last thirty days and looking closely at your own heart, ask yourself what it might take for you to become a man or woman after God's own heart. Write about that below.

DESIGNED AND QUALIFIED

When Samuel went to Jesse's house to anoint the new king, no one expected it to be David. Even Samuel believed the king was "certainly" standing in front of him—but David was still out in the field, tending the flock (see 1 Sam. 16:1-11). God reminded Samuel not to look at the outward appearance because "the LORD sees the heart" (v. 7). After all other options were exhausted, Samuel asked "Are these all the sons you have?" (v. 11). And Jesse brought David before Him.

Maybe others didn't see David and think "king," but God did—and that's what mattered. God had designed David and qualified Him to be exactly who he was.

The timeline below shows a brief summary of the story of David's life, from the moment he first came onto the scene in Scripture until his last breath.

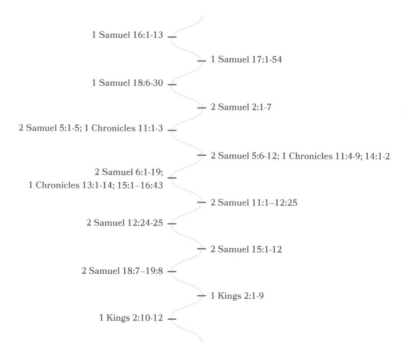

1 Samuel 16:1-13

1 Samuel 17:1-54

1 Samuel 18:6-30

2 Samuel 2:1-7

2 Samuel 5:1-5; 1 Chronicles 11:1-3

2 Samuel 5:6-12; 1 Chronicles 11:4-9; 14:1-2

2 Samuel 6:1-19;
1 Chronicles 13:1-14; 15:1–16:43

2 Samuel 11:1–12:25

2 Samuel 12:24-25

2 Samuel 15:1-12

2 Samuel 18:7–19:8

1 Kings 2:1-9

1 Kings 2:10-12

Review the passages on the timeline (p. 110) and write a few words to describe what was going on in David's life in each passage.

Now, plot some of the major events in your own life up to this point using the blank timeline below.

Even though David wasn't perfect, God called him and said David was a man after His own heart (see Acts 13:22). God gave David the strength and wisdom to lead in His perfect timing. David experienced a lot of heartbreak before getting to the throne that God had promised—and he experienced heartache after. It might not seem like God has a plan for us where we are right now, but He does, so we hold on to hope in His goodness and grace. We keep taking each step He sets before us, trusting in His design for our lives.

LIFEWAY STUDENT DEVOTIONS
Engage with God's Word.

lifeway.com/teendevotionals

☐ **THE ESSENTIALS**

☐ **CALLED**

☐ **PRESENCE & PURPOSE**

☐ **REVEALED**

☐ **LION OF JUDAH**

☐ **YOUR WILL BE DONE**

☐ **SPIRIT & TRUTH**

☐ **THREE-IN-ONE**

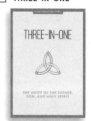

☐ **IN THE BEGINNING**

☐ **TRUTH AND LOVE**

☐ **SEARCH AND KNOW**

☐ **TAKE UP AND FOLLOW**